JESUIT LETTERS
FROM CHINA
1583-84

A Publication from
THE JAMES FORD BELL LIBRARY
at the University of Minnesota

JESUIT LETTERS FROM CHINA 1583-84

M. Howard Rienstra
Editor and Translator

UNIVERSITY OF MINNESOTA PRESS
MINNEAPOLIS

Published by the University of Minnesota Press,
2037 University Avenue Southeast, Minneapolis, MN 55414
Published simultaneously in Canada
by Fitzhenry & Whiteside Limited, Markham.
Printed in the United States of America.

Library of Congress Cataloging-in-Publication Data

Avvisi della Cina dell'ottantatre et dell'ottantaquattro.
English.
Jesuit Letters from China, 1583–84.
Translation of: Avvisi della Cina dell'ottantatre et ottanta-
quattro.
Bibliography: p.
1. Jesuits—Missions—China—History. 2. China—
History—Ming dynasty, 1368-1644—History. 3. Ruggieri,
Michele. 4. Pasio, Francesco. 5. Missionaries—China—
Correspondence. I. Rienstra, M. Howard. II. Title.
BV3417.A9613   1985   266'.251   85-8539
ISBN 0-8166-1431-8

The University of Minnesota
is an equal-opportunity
educator and employer.

To Edwin J. Van Kley

Contents

AVVISI
DELLA CINA
DELL'OTTANTATRE,
ET DELL'OTTANTA-
QVATTRO.

Come alcuni della Compagnia sono entrati dentro a terra ferma: & di alcune primitie del Christianesimo: & della speranza che v'è di progresso.

Di vna del P. Michele Ruggiero Napolitano delli 7. di Febraro. 1583. dalla Città di Sciauchino.

DOPO l'hauere io alcuni anni atteso nel porto di Amacano (doue negotiano i mercáti Portughesi) ad imparare quella sorte di lingua, che chiamano mádarina, vsata da questi Magistrati, & Cortigiani(& per vna quasi infinita quantità di charatteri, tanto difficile, che gl'istessi Cinesi vi spendono gli anni) andai alcune volte có
li

JESUIT LETTERS
FROM CHINA
1583-84

Introduction

n December of 1582 two Jesuit missionaries, Michele Ruggieri and Francesco Pasio, took up residence on mainland China in the city of Chao ch'ing. They were not the first Christian missionaries on mainland China, and their initial stay was brief, but their presence symbolized the opening of previously impenetrable China to the Christian gospel. The dream of Francis Xavier, the founder of Jesuit missions to the Far East, seemed about to be fulfilled. Europe would learn of this entry into China only from the letters of the missionaries who accomplished it. Although some letters may have arrived earlier, we know with certainty that the letters describing what was happening in China during 1583 and 1584 had all arrived in Rome by December of 1585, three years after the first residence was established. Eight of those letters were edited, abridged, and published in 1586, and are here translated into English for the first time.

Francis Xavier had sailed to the East Indies in 1541, the year after the Society of Jesus was formally founded in Rome by Ignatius Loyola and his colleagues. The remarkable success that had accompanied Xavier's gospel preaching throughout India and the Moluccas gradually led him to embrace the entire Orient in his vision for the spread of Christianity to the "greater glory of God." Thus he was drawn to Japan and arrived there in 1549. But already in February of 1548, in a letter written to Loyola, he resolved to include China in his plans. After he arrived in Japan, he came to see even more clearly the crucial importance of China, for not only was China magnificent in size, it was also the intellectual and cultural cornerstone of all oriental civilization. If Christianity is so important, the Japanese argued, why had not the Chinese, from whom they obtained their wisdom, heard of it? This haunting question gave Xavier's plan for China greater urgency. That plan, however, remained unfulfilled when he died on 2 December 1552 on Shang Ch'uan Island, off the south China coast, where he had gone to await transportation to enter the mainland.

The year of Xavier's death, 1552, was also the year when his first letters mentioning China were published in Europe. The Jesuits rather quickly discovered that publishing the letters of missionaries, and particularly those of Xavier, had considerable propaganda value, and that there was an avid reading public whose interests they satisfied. The first Letterbooks came from India, but they were not exclusively about India. In fact sixteen of the India Letterbooks published between 1552 and 1582 contain letters mentioning China, and of those sixteen, nine were published in Italian, three in Spanish, three in French and one in English.[1] The peak years for the publishing of India Letterbooks were from 1556 to 1562, after which the interest began to shift to Japan. China was mentioned in a 1570 Japan Letterbook published in Portuguese, as well as in a 1575 Japan Letterbook published in Spanish. China does not seem to have been mentioned in any subsequent Japan Letterbooks of the next decade, which were numerous. Between 1578 and 1585 twenty-two Japan Letterbooks were published in Europe: nine in Italian, nine in French, two in German, one in Spanish, and one in Latin.

European readers might well have expected the appearance

in 1586 of another of the annual Japan Letterbooks.[2] This one, however, was different. The first 168 pages of the volume contained the usual letters from Japan, but they were followed by twenty pages of abridged texts of the first eight letters from China, accounts of the work of Ruggieri and his colleague Matteo Ricci. This was news! Since we live in an age of almost instantaneous communications we have difficulty imagining a world in which information about events that happened two years previously could be regarded as news, but such was the world of 1586. Europeans read these letters from the missionaries actually living in the great kingdom of China with the same sense of freshness and immediacy we receive from today's news. The interest of European readers may again be demonstrated by the publication data. Five separate editions of this volume were published in 1586: three in Italian, one in French, and one in German.

The appearance of this 1586 Letterbook should be seen in the broader context of a steadily growing European interest in and awareness of both Japan and China. Two events of 1585 illustrate this context. The first was the celebrated visit of four young Japanese envoys to Europe. They had arrived in Lisbon in August of 1584 and gradually made their way to Rome, attracting the curious everywhere they went. They were finally received in a public consistory by Pope Gregory XIII in March of 1585.[3] Japan became a living presence in Europe in the embassy of these four young men. And their presence led to publications. At least twenty-seven separate editions of the report on the consistory were published in 1585 and 1586: eleven in Italian, nine in French, four in Latin, and three in German. That so many editions appeared in less than two years is an obvious indication of widespread interest in the Orient. Publishers were prospering from it.

Then, as if by coincidence, the second event occurred. The Augustinian Juan González de Mendoza published his *History . . . of the Grand Kingdom of China* in Rome in 1585.[4] This account of the size, the customs, the religions, and the political structure of China was based in part on previously published sources, but most significantly on unpublished accounts of the partial and temporary penetration of China by two Augustinians in 1577, and by Franciscans in 1579 and 1581. Although they were soon expelled, these Augustinians and Franciscans, who entered mainland China by way of the Philippines, did have claims to priority over the Jesuits. Half of Mendoza's book was devoted to their visits, and his preface, added after most of the book was in type, emphasized their precedence. The Augustinian wanted readers to recognize the Augustinians' lead in China missions even though he explicitly acknowledged the influence of Francis Xavier. Mendoza's book was the most important sixteenth-century contribution to European knowledge about China, and in the years 1585 and 1586 alone it appeared in twelve editions: eight in Italian and four in Spanish. One of the Italian editions is quite curious. As an addendum to Mendoza's text, the publisher printed the same eight Jesuit letters from China that were being published in the Japan Letterbook of 1586.[5] The Jesuits got their notices published in an otherwise Augustinian book.

Sixteenth-century Letterbooks present readers with some perplexing problems. The letters were not published as written by the missionaries. The secretary of the Society of Jesus in Rome was primarily responsible for editing the letters for publication, but undoubtedly enlisted others in the complex process of translating, abbreviating, and censoring. They were commonly translated from Spanish or Portuguese into Italian, a process complicated by the difficulties the missionaries themselves had in finding Western terminology to express Asian institutions and ideas. Since the letters contained much administrative detail that would be of little interest to general readers, they were almost always abridged. Only a careful comparison of the printed version and the original manuscript can reveal precisely what transformations occurred in the process of publishing each letter. Not all of the problems can be attributed to the editors, however. The missionaries themselves often displayed what Donald F. Lach has called "excessive zeal in reporting the initial success of the mission."[6] As early as 1566, the reliability of the

Letterbooks was being questioned by the Jesuits themselves, and the Japan Letterbooks did not escape such criticism even in 1586, although the major defects were usually corrected by that time.

For the eight letters from China, however, the situation is somewhat different. Since most of these letters were written in Italian, there were few initial translating difficulties. Nor did these letters from China exaggerate the successes of the mission. Rather they carefully indicated how tenuous the Jesuits' situation was, and claimed very modest results. While emphasizing the long-range importance of the acceptance that had been accorded the missionaries by the Chinese authorities, the letters candidly noted that only two baptisms had been performed. This was in marked contrast to the reports from Japan of tens of thousands of baptisms. But the letters from China were also abridged, in fact radically so in some instances, and they too were censored. In the notes to the translations I have indicated some of the more significant differences between the original and published versions of the letters.

These variant readings seem to be of three kinds. First there are the abridgments that eliminated administrative detail. These seem to be based on simple and straightforward judgments by the editor of what would not likely be interesting to the general reading public. Slightly more complex are the deletions of material that, although probably of interest to general readers, might not be understood by them. Some of these concern the structure of Chinese society, which only modern critical scholarship, using Chinese sources to complement the Western, has managed to untangle and explain. The sixteenth-century editor may also have chosen to delete material that he had difficulty understanding. But the third and most troublesome type of variant reading is due to censorship.

The Jesuits published these Letterbooks, it must be remembered, not as acts of disinterested historical scholarship, but to promote interest in and support for their missionary endeavors. Caught up in the enthusiasm, as well as the difficulty, of their work, the missionaries often wrote things that could easily be misunderstood in the context of European Christianity. These first missionaries to China had the great difficulty of explaining why the gospel had to be "accommodated" to Chinese culture. Given the prevailing European attitudes of racial and cultural superiority, this was no easy task. Michele Ruggieri and Matteo Ricci clearly perceived that for the gospel to be successfully propagated in China, the missionaries would have to become Chinese, but could European readers understand and accept this? This question seems to lie behind most of the obvious examples of censorship of these letters. The words that the missionaries used were changed, not translated. The European editor wanted to convey the idea of a triumphant and culturally superior Christianity, whereas the missionaries were writing of the necessity of a cultural transformation of European Christianity to a Chinese setting. We must be careful not to read into this censorship the controversies about accommodation that emerged in the Rites Controversy of the following century, but that debate was certainly being anticipated in 1586. However valid and appropriate the method of cultural accommodation may have been to the first successes of Christianity in China, it is also true that in 1586 Ricci's use of the term could have aroused as much suspicion and contention as it did in the seventeenth century.

The modern reader of these letters, therefore, is obliged to read them as they were published but must also learn what contemporary critical scholarship can reveal about what was not published. Both give the reader insights into China and Europe in the 1580s.

The China of the late 1580s which the Jesuits entered was that of the late Ming dynasty (1368–1644). Although the country was generally closed to foreigners, its geographical magnitude and immense population had already captured the imagination of generations of literate Europeans. Curiously, they managed to overestimate the size of China, but nothing could have led them to overestimate its population. They apparently thought that China extended northward to the 50th parallel of latitude, a figure corrected to the 42d parallel in the early years of the seventeenth century. We now know that late Ming China comprised a territory of some twenty-four degrees latitude and some thirty degrees longitude. Grand, but not quite as grand as Europe had thought in the 1580s. Literate Europeans had long been accustomed to the "millions" described by Marco Polo, but they would have been incredulous if faced with the best modern population estimate for late Ming China of 150 million persons.[7]

The era of the 1580s in China was that of the Wan-li emperor whose personal name was Shen-tsung (1572–1620). The Wan-li emperor was notoriously avaricious, reclusive, and inattentive

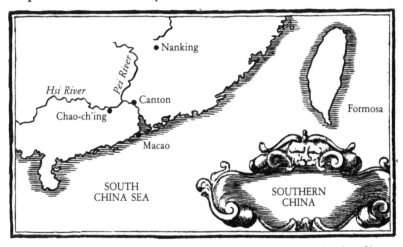

to matters of governing. He ruled from Peking with the direct assistance of a bureaucracy that consisted of three grand secretaries, six boards of ministry, a censorate, and five generals. A recurring problem of the imperial government in Ming times was the power exercised by the court eunuchs. The Wan-li emperor's inattention to governing allowed these eunuchs, members of the personal household of the emperor, to attain more power than ever before, to compromise the highest levels of the bureaucracy, and to arbitrarily disrupt the functioning of government from the imperial to the local levels.

The second level of government in Ming China was provincial. There were fifteen provinces: thirteen were regional provinces, but two had a slightly higher dignity as provinces of the two imperial capital cities, Nanking and Peking, and were called metropolitan provinces. To administer this provincial structure, Peking appointed viceroys, known as Supreme Commanders (tsung-tu), and governors, known as Grand Coordinators (hsün fu). The governors represented imperial policies and interests in single provinces, whereas the viceroys supervised two or more provinces. There were also imperial commissioners (tu-t'ang) in all the major cities. The emperor and the Peking bureaucracy ensured itself imperial control by appointing these officials and myriads of lower local officials as well.[8]

The Jesuits entered Kwangtung, the southernmost province. The governor of that province resided in Canton, the capital city. There was also a viceroy resident in Chao ch'ing. The Jesuits sought out and dealt with the viceroy, the governor, and several imperial commissioners. During the period covered by these letters they never ventured outside Kwangtung province. There they dealt successfully with the viceroy and others, but they had little understanding of how the entire imperial structure worked, and they knew virtually nothing about what was happening in that remote northern imperial city of Peking.

The letters from China, beginning with the 3 February 1583 letter of Michele Ruggieri, presented the immediate background to the Jesuit entry into China. As noted previously, there had been earlier attempts to penetrate Ming China, but this finally successful attempt by the Jesuits was launched from Macao and can almost be dated to the appointment of Alessandro Valignano as Visitor to the east in 1573, and his arrival in India in 1574. Macao was a Portuguese trading entrepôt on a peninsula off the southern coast of China, apparently obtained by the Portuguese in return for their assistance in clearing the coastal waters of pirates. The college of Jesuits in Macao ministered to the nine hundred Portuguese, and to those few of the larger population of Chinese who became Christians. These Chinese were quickly "Europeanized."[9] They were compelled to dress like Europeans and to take European names. Valignano thought this inappropriate for any successful Christian mission to China because of its ancient, sophisticated civilization. He also recognized that the Jesuits in Macao were totally committed to Europeanization and thus provided little hope for a successful mission to mainland China. Valignano, therefore, sent to Goa for new personnel, and the response was the arrival of Michele Ruggieri in Macao in July 1579.

Ruggieri immediately began to study Chinese. The other Jesuits had relied on Chinese translators. Learning the language was so demanding that he did not participate in any of the Macao ministries, and thus he incurred the resentment of the other Jesuits. In November of 1580 he wrote that some of them were murmuring as follows: "What is the sense of this Father occupying himself with this sort of thing when he could be of service to other ministries of the Society? It is a waste of time for him to learn the Chinese language and to consecrate himself to a hopeless enterprise."[10] But with the support and encouragement of Valignano, he persisted.

In 1580 Ruggieri accompanied the Portuguese merchants to Canton on one of their semiannual trading missions, and he began then to ingratiate himself with the Chinese authorities. Perhaps because of his evident respect for their language and their culture, and because of his pleasant and astute manners, he was able to inaugurate Valignano's program. The tentative beginnings in the process of accommodating Christianity to Chinese culture had been made. Two other persons were soon to join Ruggieri. They too were Italian and had sailed from Lisbon to Goa with Ruggieri in 1578. The first, Francesco Pasio, was with Ruggieri in Chao ch'ing, but upon their expulsion in 1583, he left permanently for Japan. The other was Matteo Ricci.

Ricci would become the much more famous successor to Ruggieri, but in the immediate context of these letters he is still Ruggieri's follower. Matteo Ricci's name is virtually synonymous with the success of the Jesuits in China, and rightly so. However, he did not arrive in Macao until August of 1582 and then plunged immediately into the study of Chinese with Ruggieri. His first trip to Chao ch'ing was in September of 1583 in the company of Ruggieri. By virtue of his linguistic abilities and his complete commitment to Valignano's program of cultural respect and accommodation, he was the best possible companion and successor to Ruggieri. The reader in 1586, however, would not have known that Ruggieri would soon return to Europe and that Ricci would continue to work in China until his death in 1610.

This first English translation of the letters attempts to preserve some of the sense and character of their earliest published version, but with one major difference. The sentences have been shortened. Through the use of such relative pronouns as "il che" and "il quale," sixteenth-century Italian sentences could run on almost indefinitely. I have frequently used their appearance in a sentence as an opportunity to start a new sentence by repeating the major noun. I have not used brackets or parentheses to indicate this change. Brackets are used only when I have interpolated a word not in the text, and parentheses are used only when they were in the original. Other clarifications of the text are usually based on comparisons with the original letters as published by Tacchi Venturi and interpreted by the scholar Pasquala D'Elia,[11] and are included in the accompanying notes.

THE LETTERS

The Letters

ow some of the Company have entered upon the mainland; of some of the first fruits of Christianity; and of the hope there is for progress.

From a letter of Father Michele Ruggieri,
Neapolitan, the seventh of
February, 1583, from the city
of Chao ch'ing

I spent some years in the port of Macao, where the Portuguese merchants do their trading, learning the language which they call Mandarin. It is the language used by these magistrates and courtiers which, because of an almost infinite quantity of characters, is so difficult that the Chinese themselves spend years at it. On several occasions I went with those Portuguese merchants to the city of Canton, about seventy miles from Macao. They are permitted for three months each year to engage in trade there, but in such a manner that they are not permitted to lodge on land; such is the caution with which this people treats foreigners. Nevertheless, it pleased our Lord God the first time I went *that I would find favor in the sight of Pharoah*,[1] that is, with one of those whom they call Mandarins who govern the city. Having spoken with him several times and noticing how he seemed so favorably and affectionately disposed toward me, I put a supplication to him that I be allowed to live on the land since it was not permissible for me to perform my sacrifices on the water. He issued a memorial, ordering that I be given a small house, and commanding under threat of life that no one should cause me any harm. Day and night many, many people came simply to see me. There were so many that they broke an opening in the wall of the house. Through this opening a certain one—I don't know by what spirit he was moved— entered, and with his own hands took a rock and gave himself three blows to the head, shedding his blood throughout the house. He then left, screaming that I had wounded him so as to arouse the people against me. But our Lord God turned everything to the good and gave me greater determination to pursue the undertaking. For the Mandarin, having called me to him, asked if I had wounded him. And when I responded, "No," he added, "I believe you since I know him to be a wicked man." I stayed in that house for three consecutive months, saying Mass publicly for the Portuguese. Some of the Lord Mandarins and lawyers visited me, gave me some small tokens of their charity, and informed themselves about our doctrines by asking many questions. Thus they acquired still greater familiarity, and the common people gave me respect. And all this happened the first time I went to Canton.[2]

The second time I went there, I was assigned a better house by the supreme magistrate (who is like a viceroy and is called the *tu-t'ang*).[3] This is the greatest marvel of all since in years past in the court of this same *tu-t'ang* there had been issued an order prohibiting the admission of any of our fathers. This was because of a Chinese who had become a Christian in Macao.[4] With the favor thus shown me by the *tu-t'ang*, the other Mandarins also gave me their friendship. Among them was a general of the army to whom I gave a clock. He wanted very much to lodge me even further inland. I lived in this house during my second and third visits while the Portuguese attended to their business aboard their ships.

I returned the fourth time upon the occasion of the arrival of a new *tu-t'ang* who had orders, or so it seemed to him, to drive the Portuguese out of the kingdom. To that end, he sent for the mayor and the bishop of Macao, who did not dare go. But it seemed to the Father Visitor[5] that I should go (as I did) with a Portuguese auditor[6] and accompanied by a servant of the *tu-t'ang*. The *tu-t'ang* seemed very agitated that the Portuguese were staying in that port and city without the license of his king, threatening that we had not yet experienced his power and force. Then all at once he had the three hundred men of his guard, standing in two ranks, unsheath their swords. But, seeing that we responded calmly and serenely, and that our manner was to treat the Chinese as brothers and without offense, he first calmed himself down and then even favored us with banquets and presents, and offered to help us with the king. We busied ourselves there for the space of fifteen days, with the entire city marveling at the reception given us. Then, taking our leave, we returned to Macao.

On another occasion the people of Macao sent the same auditor with a present, and since I was gravely ill with an acute fever the *tu-t'ang* asked about me. The auditor replied that I was very sick, for which the *tu-t'ang* showed deep concern, and presented him some eyeglasses on my behalf, telling him that when I was cured I should return and bring him a very beautiful iron clock. He seemed very pleased that I had remembered him and told the auditor that he would see to it that I could come there and bring the clock. And since I was delayed due to convalescence, he confirmed the matter by a letter of his own. Whence it seemed to the Father Visitor that we should not lose this opportunity to ask for a fixed residence and to continue the study of the language. Father Francesco Pasio was given to me as my companion, and we arrived two days after Christmas, 1582.[7]

We were received with much tenderness. Once, upon going to visit the *tu-t'ang*, he asked us if we feared the Demon and if we had a remedy to cast him out. We responded that by the grace of our Lord God we have no fear of him, and that by the power of the same Lord, he flees. He had asked this because in a very important city where he used to live the Demon showed himself in terrifying visions. This *tu-t'ang*, by virtue of his greater authority, allowed us on rare occasions to observe the practices of their magistrates, practices which are no small impediment to the goals to which we aspire. Happily he gave us his very lovable secretary, with whom we should deal whenever we would have need. He sent us things to eat, and sometimes money. Through him we presented the clock to the *tu-t'ang*. It pleased him very much as a thing of much ingenuity and completely new to China.[8] We think he sent it to the king.

One time, among others, as we were visiting him, and finding him in a good mood, we put forth our request for a residence inside China, both to learn their language and letters, and to share ours with them. It pleased the goodness of God that he would accept our request. He gave us a house, quite secluded and suitable to our purposes.[9] Further, a license was obtained so that Father Matteo Ricci might enter as my third companion, and thus he was sent for. There is no doubt that the Father Visitor is most thankful to the goodness of God for the grace and mercy given us in so difficult a matter. It was previously thought to be impossible to be able to enter into this grand kingdom, which in the forty years since our good Father Francis Xavier began the undertaking, has not been accomplished until now. May the Lord, in whom our hope is placed, be thanked forever. And we desire the help of the prayers of Your Paternity, of all the Company of Europe, and particularly of Rome, in whose college all three of us were students together. We do not know what the *tu-t'ang* will do with us, especially when he comes to the end of his reign in another two

years. We are saying to the Lord, *"Prepare my heart, oh God.*
. . . "[10] The *tu-t'ang* is pleased with the good relations he has
had with us, that we have studied and understand mathemat-
ics, and that we can make ingenious things such as sun clocks
and other things having to do with the sphere. In this regard
he said one day that such knowledge serves God and is thus a
wonderful thing. This is because they call the Heavens God,
which they adore supremely. It was, he said, convenient to
grant residence to persons useful to the republic. He was able
to do this by virtue of a particular privilege granted him by the
king, but not left to the discretion of the other *tu-t'angs*; that
is, either to admit or to drive out the Portuguese. At the moment we are attempting, with the favor of God, to edify these
Gentiles by the example of our life, and hoping that our interpreters will do the same.[11] We are still learning to read better
and to understand their books in order to refute their errors.
Your Paternity would favor us by devoting some Masses to this
mission, and by some of your letters to console us and to direct
us in the Divine service.

From a letter of Father Francesco Pasio,
Bolognese, the twenty-seventh of
June, 1583 [from Macao]

In the past Your Paternity has learned how we entered
into China. Now I will tell you how it happened, because of my
sins, that news came to the *tu-t'ang* of Canton from the Royal
City of Peking that he had fallen into disgrace with the king
and has been deprived of his office. Therefore, we have been
told that on no account are we able to remain in China any
longer. We searched for all possible ways to remain at least until
the arrival of his successor, but it was not possible. Thus we find
ourselves once again in this port of Macao, confident in the Lord
that our stay inside the kingdom will not have been without
some fruit. Therefore, with the experience we have acquired in

the land, our familiarity and acceptance by the Gentiles, we hope that it will be easier to obtain a license to return from the new *tu-t'ang*.

From a letter of Father Francesco Cabral,[12] Superior at the House of Macao, the twentieth of November, 1583

❧ Seeing how the *tu-t'ang* was deposed and our fathers were sent back to this port of Macao, one of them, Father Francesco Pasio, went to Japan. Father Matteo Ricci stayed here as a companion of Father Ruggieri, awaiting that which our Lord God would graciously be pleased to do about this mission to China. It pleased His infinite goodness that when we were least expecting it, that is, three months after having returned, there came a Chinese from Chao ch'ing, a city of fifty thousand households and inland some fifty leagues from Macao, where the *tu-t'ang* resides. He came with a passport from the Cescien,[13] who is like a protector of the land, to call our fathers to him in order to inform himself what it is they hope to accomplish. For that reason it seemed that the same fathers, Michele Ruggieri and Matteo Ricci, ought to be sent together with a good interpreter. And we others remain, commending the mission to the Lord. Through His mercy they found the said protector so favorably disposed that they obtained their license from the new *tu-t'ang*. They are allowed to remain and to live inside the country. And he gave them a site to build a house and a church. For all this we rest comforted in the Lord.

From another letter of Father Michele
Ruggieri, from Macao, the twenty-
fifth of January, 1584

ЖФ By others of my letters Your Paternity will have understood how it was pleasing to the goodness of God to open for
us anew the door to be able to enter into this grand kingdom
of China by sending me to call upon the new *tu-t'ang*. He, having understood how we have come from that Company of Rome
sent by the Great Father, that is, by the Highest Pontiff, and
seeing that we have desired to learn their language and their letters in order to be able reciprocally to share ours with them,
received me very lovingly. He gave me the choice of a site in
the better part of the city on which to build a house for me and
my companions, and a chapel in which to say Mass. Further, he
gave me a license to be able to teach the Chinese, some of
whom loaned me a hundred scudi for that beginning.[14] That
sum, in relation to the great abundance of all things here, is of
no small moment as it would be there.[15] With this [loan], and
with some other help, the small house was built in which Father
Matteo Ricci and I live, together with some interpreters who as-
sist us. The [Chinese] lords visit us continually and show great
affection toward us. Whence we place our trust in the help of
our Lord, who, as He had deigned to begin this work to His
great glory, so also will He give us the light and grace to continue it according to His most holy will. I have come here to
Macao to seek some contributions from the Portuguese to finish
the chapel. With these Chinese one needs to proceed with great
adroitness and suavity, and not with indiscreet fervor. Otherwise it would be very easy to close the door that God our Lord
has opened to us, and I don't know when it would be opened
again. I say this because the people are enemies of foreigners,
and especially of Christians, seeing them as companies sur-
rounded by Portuguese and Castilians whom they consider bel-
licose men.[16] Wherefore, if others would attempt to enter, they
would not be able to do so without seeking a license from these

would not be able to do so without seeking a license from thse magistrates. Doing it in any other manner would result in their being expelled, and we with them.

With that which I am gaining in the language, and with the help here that increases every day,[17] I have finished reviewing the Catechism in the Chinese language that I began four years ago. And it pleases these Chinese governing lords so much that they have compelled me to print it.[18]

From another letter of the same [Michele Ruggieri], from Chao ch'ing, the thirtieth of May, 1584

We are devoting ourselves, as has already been written, to learning these letters, and to sacrificing in our chapel of the Madonna here in Chao ch'ing.[19] We do so in the hope that with time our Lord God will bring forth fruit from this uncultivated land. We do not wish for now to baptize, even though there are several who seek it, in order to allow them to grow more in the knowledge and desire of things Divine, and in order not to give occasion to the Demon if some would then leave the faith in these beginning [times].[20] We are starting to win and to instruct some who will serve as interpreters. They will benefit us with their work when the time comes to preach the holy Gospel to this poor people. The Mandarins love us and are very content with our staying here.[21] One of the most learned of them composed some verses and sent them to me, together with two titles written on gilded tablets. The one is to be placed above the door of our house, and the other in the chapel.[22] For the consolation of our [brethren], I put them here as they sound in our language.

Titles

Church and New Flower of the Saints
From the West there came to us, Fathers, Men Most Pure[23]

Verses

Let us give a song to the heavenly man.
From the western Kingdom, carried in a small ship
   for ten thousand miles, he crossed the vast ocean.
Only because he was human did he enter the celebrated
   solitude of the Chinese, that as holy man he might rest
there.
In the dead of night a dragon descends into the lake:
   all around the violent wave grows dark.
When spring comes a guò bird is sent out
   into the wooded, green field.
Here he is forgetful of himself and his own;
   does he remember his dear place of birth?
As his heart knows the right, so alone he pours
   forth prayers to God, and reads books.
He came to see in the region situated in the middle,
   men preparing for themselves a road to Heaven.
How rare the man with strong and resolute mind
   who would spread forth an odor far and wide.[24]

From another letter of the same [Michele Ruggieri], from Macao, the twenty-first of October, 1584

It has pleased our Lord God that our lovable protector from Chao ch'ing[25] has been confirmed for three more years by the king, with an increase in honors and powers. This is the one who has favored and helped us, and who had made for our house and chapel those titles and verses about which I wrote in my other letter. Chinese of all ranks openly come into our chapel to adore the holy images, to ask about Christian doctrine and about that holy water which cancels sins (which is how they describe baptism). But we restrain them so that they may be better instructed and rooted in the desire for eternal salvation. This year there have come from Peking, the Royal City, ten books of the histories of this grand kingdom which are very authentic. We will study them and make extracts from them in order to send them to Your Paternity next year, since, by the grace of the Lord, both of us already know how to read and to understand these writings, and even to speak with mediocrity. I have returned here to Macao, having received a license from the prefect of Chao ch'ing that Father Francesco Cabral, superior of the house of Macao and our [Superior] of the residence in Chao ch'ing, might come to visit it in order to console us and direct us in our actions to the greater glory of God. We will leave for that purpose in five or six days.

From a letter of Father Matteo Ricci,
Maceratese, the thirtieth of
November, 1584, from the
city of Canton

✠ I have come here from our residence in Chao ch'ing for several things suggested to me by Father Michele Ruggieri. The Catechism that we have made and printed in the Chinese language, by the grace of the Lord, has been very well received.[26] In it, by means of a dialogue between a Gentile and a Father from Europe, there are presented all the things necessary to be a Christian in good order, good letters, and good language.[27] In it the principal sects of China are refuted,[28] and there are the Ten Commandments, the Pater Noster, and the Ave Maria.

The prefect had me make a map in the manner of ours of Europe, but with the distances and names of countries in the Chinese language.[29] And he immediately printed it without my reviewing it or thinking that it would be sent to press. He esteems it so much that he keeps the print with him, not wanting anyone to learn about it except those to whom he slowly presents it, the more important persons of China. The building of our little house in Chao ch'ing is almost finished, and although it is small, all the nobility come to see it — so much so that we have no rest. This year the prefect that has been so favorable to us has been made *limsitao*,[30] that is, governor of many cities. This should be no little help at the proper time for the propagation of the Gospel.

We have experienced many tribulations, even to the point of being accused falsely of very serious things at the suggestion of the ancient adversary.[31] *But from all this God has freed us so that His name may be blessed throughout the ages.*[32]

From a letter of Father Francesco
Cabral, Portuguese, from
Macao, on the eighth
of December, 1584

In this I will give a summary to Your Paternity of my going to Chao ch'ing, from which, after staying there several days, I have returned two days ago. I was with those two Fathers of ours who, as you well know, have often written me from there that it would not be possible to get a license to permit me to come. Nevertheless, it pleased the Lord that one be obtained from the *limsitao*, who is that prefect about whom we have written at other times. There was no doubt that because of his good deportment and wise governance, he would be promoted elsewhere to some higher office, as are promoted all those who in their three-year office conduct themselves well. For our cause this would not be a small disturbance. But it pleased Divine providence that when the principal persons of Chao ch'ing wrote to the court that they would not wish to be cut off from a man of such valor, he was promoted in the same city of Chao ch'ing to the next higher dignity after the viceroy, which is called *limsitao*, before whom the prefect, the magistracy he had before, bows. Therefore, when the license was obtained from him, Father Ruggieri came for me and we went together. Father Ricci awaited us with great eagerness. It was most comforting to all three of us to see each other together in the midst of that people. The following day some of the principals of the city came to visit me. Knowing that the *limsitao* had given me a passport, all of them presented themselves to me with much cordiality, praying that I would not depart so quickly, and that I would stay at least a couple of months.

One day later Father Ruggieri and I went to pay homage to the *limsitao*. He was pleased with my coming and put some questions to me in a pleasant manner. He then dismissed me, saying that he would send someone to visit me.[33] He did just that after three or four hours, when through one of his captains he told me that I was welcome and gave me a present of the kind given to similarly highly esteemed persons. There was a piece of white silk cloth, six fans, and four of those maps by Father Matteo, saved to be given to friends or else to Father Ruggieri.[34] This was quickly known throughout the city, and some of the principals came to congratulate us for the honor and the compliments that the *limsitao* gave us. Wherefore the common people dare not treat us badly, as they do the ministers of their idols, for whom they have little esteem.[35]

The day of the Presentation of the Madonna I baptized two Chinese, who were the first to become Christians inside China. The one was a nobleman and lettered. He had gone to the court of the king, where he hoped to be made a Mandarin for having that degree of literature that is desired for such an office. He had been in our house for four or five months, helping the Fathers put the Catechism into the Chinese language. By these conversations, and by the continual reading and copying of the Catechism, he was illuminated by the Lord. He begged me, with much insistence, to baptize him. Then, when he was suffi-

ciently instructed in the matters of our holy faith, I did it with
the approval of these Fathers. And he was called Paul. At the
same time I baptized another citizen of Chao ch'ing, a married
man, to whom was given the name John. He had been the first
to receive our [Fathers] in his house, and upon that occasion
had been well catechized. Another who was present also wanted
to be baptized, but it seemed well to defer it for good reasons.
That which gives me great comfort, and which gives me great
hope that our Lord God will open the treasures of His mercy in
this great kingdom is that not only was the baptism of them not
taken for ill in the city and by the Mandarins, but they rejoiced
in it. And hearing about how Paul, so noble and literate, had
become a Christian, some of the principals came to congratulate him and us, saying that soon there would be others and
how pleased they were that a man so well known had taken our
law. I also place my faith in the Divine Goodness, that He will
be served much by these two grains of the first-fruits of China,
so long desired by our Company and all the servants of the
Lord. The day following the baptism John came to tell us that
all the people of his street were moved to become Christians,
having understood that he had done so. Paul, who is of the
province of Fukien, will stop by his home on the way to the
court (at Peking) and intends to make Christians of his wife and
children and to teach all of them the law of God. To that end,
he is taking with him some of the Catechisms already printed.
May the Lord guide his steps.[36]

That city where we have been given license to live is a place
more suited to spread the Gospel, in my view, than there is in
all of China from the Royal City on down. Since the *tu-t'ang*
always resides in Chao ch'ing, all the Mandarins of this province
necessarily return there because of the custom and obligation
they have to visit him at the beginning of each month, although those who live far away usually come every two months.
And all, when finishing the three-year term of their office, before returning to the court of the king, must come to be licensed by him. And similarly, those who come from the court,
provided with new assignments and duties, render him obe-

dience before taking possession of them. And they usually come to our house to see this novel thing in China. Here they are shown some things of Europe which to them are unusual and strange, such as triangular crystals (prisms), the map with Chinese letters, and other things in which they take delight.[37] This gives us the opportunity to deal familiarly with them and to share our affections in such a manner that our fame has already spread through the greater part of China, and they take more notice of us than of the ministers of idols. And insofar as I have understood the ease with which these Gentiles hear the things of our holy faith, it is to be hoped that the Lord has reserved for us a great harvest in this spacious land, if we on our part, with all humility and desiring the honor of the blessed Christ, dispose ourselves to cultivate it as it should be. I, after having given some instructions to our Fathers, was licensed by the *limsitao*. He gave me another passport and gave orders to a Mandarin that I should be given a boat of the king's guard. I will save the said passport to be used when I happen to return to Chao ch'ing.

The Mandarin language in this port of Macao, because of a lack of expert teachers, seems much more difficult. Now Father Matteo Ricci, who has learned it well and made notes on it, tells me that he thinks six months would be enough time to teach it to our brothers (given that they have the talent and use it diligently) to such a degree that they could understand it, and be understood. It is true that the pronunciation is painful and one cannot learn it so quickly.[38]

It remains only to pray Your Paternity that you intercede much with our Lord God for this mission that is so important to His holy service and to the salvation of many thousands of souls, who, for the lack of those who will show them the way of salvation, will perish miserably.

APPENDIX

Appendix

he eight letters published in 1586, and here translated into English for the first time, are abbreviated parts of a corpus of forty extant letters written by Ruggieri and associates that relate to the beginnings of the China mission. They were all written from the spring of 1579 to the end of 1584, and most were addressed to the generals of the Jesuit Order, Mercuriano through 1581 and Acquaviva after. Father Pasquale D'Elia, *Fonti Ricciane*, I, clviii–clx, prepared a comprehensive registry of all such letters. Most of them are preserved in the Historical Archives of the Society of Jesus in Rome. The following list is based on D'Elia's registry and includes all those written to the generals of the Order by the authors of the eight letters published in 1586. The eight are indicated by italic type.

Author	*Place*	*Date*	
M. Ruggieri	Cochin	1 May	1579
M. Ruggieri	Macao	8 Nov.	1580
M. Ruggieri	Macao	8 Nov.	1580
M. Ruggieri	Macao	12 Nov.	1581
M. Ruggieri	Macao	14 Dec.	1582
F. Pasio	Chao ch'ing	5 Feb.	1583

M. Ruggieri	*Chao ch'ing*	*7 Feb.*	*1583*
M. Ricci	Macao	13 Feb.	1583
F. Pasio	*Macao*	*27 June*	*1583*
F. Cabral	*Macao*	*20 Nov.*	*1583*
M. Ruggieri	*Macao*	*25 Jan.*	*1584*
M. Ruggieri	*Chao ch'ing*	*30 May*	*1584*
F. Cabral	Macao	6 Oct.	1584
M. Ruggieri	*Macao*	*21 Oct.*	*1584*
M. Ricci	*Canton*	*30 Nov.*	*1584*
F. Cabral	*Macao*	*8 Dec.*	*1584*

There are two later letters of Michele Ruggieri, both written from Chao ch'ing. One was written on 18 October 1585 and the other on 8 November 1586. He returned to Rome in November 1588.

NOTES

Notes

Introduction

1. These and the following enumerations are based on a careful study by Robert Streit, *Bibliotheca Missionum: Asiatische Missionliteratur: 1245*-1599, vol. 4 (Aachen: 1928). The specific entries are nos.669–70.

2. For a complete bibliographical description, see the end of the Bibliography in this book.

3. The best account of this Japanese mission is to be found in Donald F. Lach, *Asia in the Making of Europe*, vol. 1, *The Century of Discovery*, bk. 2 (Chicago: University of Chicago Press, 1965), pp. 688–706.

4. For this, too, Lach is the best and most convenient source. See pp. 742–94.

5. Item no. 1987 in Streit, *Dell' Historia della China . . . si sono aggionti alcuni avisi pur della China non piu stampati in questo libro . . . Mendozza* (Genova: G. Bartoli, 1586). A copy can be found in the John Carter Brown Library. The letters are printed on pp. 271–80.

6. Lach, *Asia*, vol. 1, bk. 1, pp. 318–19.

7. Pint-ti Ho, *Studies on the Population of China, 1368-1953* (Cambridge, Mass.: Harvard University Press, 1959), pp. 257–65.

8. This account of the structure of late Ming government is based primarily on Charles O. Hucker, *The Ming Dynasty: Its Origins and Evolving Institutions* (Ann Arbor: Center for Chinese Studies, 1978).

9. For the best brief account of Europeanization, see George H.

Dunne, *Generation of Giants* (Notre Dame: University of Notre Dame Press, 1962), esp. pp. 17–19.

10. Quoted in Dunne, *Generation of Giants*, p. 19.

11. See Father Pietro Tacchi Venturi, *Le Opere Storiche del P. Matteo Ricci, S.J.* 2 vols. (Macerata: F. Giorgetti, 1911–13); and Father Pasquale M. D'Elia, S.J.,*Fonti Ricciane*, 3 vols. (Rome: La Libreria Dello Stato, 1942–49).

Translation

1. The phrase is in Latin and refers to Acts 7:10. In the original letter as edited by Father Pietro Tacchi Venturi, *Le Opere Storiche del P. Matteo Ricci, S.J.*, 2 vols. (Macerata: F. Giorgetti, 1911–13), 2, p. 413, only two Latin words, *conspectu Pharaonis*, are given and underlined, whereas in this published version there are six Latin words.

2. This published version of the letter is not as clear on the separate trips as the original is. Ruggieri visited Canton four times: in April 1580; in October and later in 1581; and in April or May 1582. Then, as this letter explains further on, Ruggieri and Pasio went to Chao ch'ing in December 1582. This letter was written from Chao ch'ing in February 1583. For the dating of the four visits, one must consult the monumental work of Father Pasquale M. D'Elia, S.J., *Fonti Ricciane*, 3 vols. (Rome: Libreria dello Stato, 1942–49). Hereafter it is cited as *Fonti Ricciane*. For a brief summary, see also Pasquale M. D'Elia, "La Reprise des Missions Catholiques en Chine a la fin des Ming,"*Journal of World History* 5 (1959–60), pp. 679–85; and Arnold H. Rowbotham, *Missionary and Mandarin: The Jesuits at the Court of China* (New York: Russell & Russell, 1966), pp. 52–57.

3. Apart from the generic use of *Mandarin*, the published letters use the Italian form *tutano* to refer to high-level Chinese officials. The proper modernization for the Chinese term is *tu-t'ang*, and I shall use this to render the Italian. However, in the original letter edited by Tacchi Venturi, Ruggieri used two terms: *aitao* and *vicerè*. "*Vicerè*" is properly used for a viceroy who is a *tu-t'ang* of each province. *Aitao*, however, is a romanized version of the Chinese title *hai-tao*. Whereas the *tu-t'ang* was a governor of a province, the *hai-tao* was a grand admiral responsible for dealing with all foreigners, piracy, and coastal defenses. The discrete use of these terms is not consistently clear in the original letter, and their meaning is completely obscured by the European editor's decision to render all such references *tutano*.

4. The original letter explains that some years earlier a Father accompanying the Portuguese to Canton had secretly transported a young convert back to Macao, thus arousing the charge of kidnapping. The lad was restored to his parents after a show of force by the Chinese authorities. Matteo Ricci in his journals was later to write, "Nothing but the ingenuity and the courteous manners of a Ruggieri could have succeeded in overcoming this difficulty and regaining their good graces." Louis J. Gallagher's translation of Trigault's edition of Ricci's journals, *China in the Sixteenth Century: The Journals of Matthew Ricci: 1583–1610* (New York: Random House, 1953), p. 133. Hereafter it is cited as Ricci-Trigault.

5. The Father Visitor was Alessandro Valignano. He was principally responsible for the encouragement and organization of the venture into China. On Valignano, see Louis Pfister, S.J., *Notices Biographiques et Bibliographiques sur les Jésuites de l'Ancienne Mission de Chine: 1552–1773* (Chang-Hai: La Mission Catholique, 1932), pp. 13–14. See also George H. Dunne, S.J., *Generation of Giants: The Story of the Jesuits in China in the Last Decades of the Ming Dynasty* (Notre Dame: University of Notre Dame Press, 1962). Dunne writes, "Valignano . . . gave entirely new direction to the enterprise," p. 17.

6. This is evidently the Italian rendering of *Ouvidor*, the Chief Judge of the Portuguese settlement at Macao. On the structure of the administration of Macao, see Tien-Tse Chang, *Sino-Portuguese Trade from 1514 to 1644* (Leyden: E. J. Brill, 1969), pp. 96–108. The auditor was Mattia Penella according to Ricci-Trigault, p. 136.

7. On Francesco Pasio, see Pfister, *Notices*, pp. 21–22, and *Fonti Ricciane*, vol. 1, p. 165, and vol 3, p. 216.

8. In a letter written from Macao on 13 February 1583, Matteo Ricci, then the newest and junior member of the trio, comments a bit more sanguinely on this gift of a clock. "Of the clock, not much is said because it is made in our manner and gives the hours diversely from theirs. They marvel more to see a machine that moves by itself and sounds the hours than as an artifice to tell time. Thus it was not the cause of this entry as has been thought." Tacchi Venturi, *Ricci*, vol. 2, p. 33.

9. This account is significantly abbreviated for a European reading public. Ruggieri wrote in the original, "He wished us to dress in the manner of their Fathers, which is a little different from ours, and now we do so dress, and, in short, we have become Chinese, *ut Christo Sinas lucrifaciamus* (so that we may gain China for Christ)." In Tacchi Venturi, *Ricci*, vol. 2, p. 416. This explicit statement of the practice of accommodating themselves to Chinese culture was apparently thought to be too

strong for a European audience in 1586. In the previously cited 13 February letter of Matteo Ricci, the circumstances of their acceptance are clarified even further. Ricci wrote that "when the Fathers said to him that they wanted to become vassals of the king of China, and that they would even change their mode of dress — all of which seemed very good to him — he said to them that he would give them the habit of the priests of Peking, which is the most honored one could give." Tacchi Venturi, *Ricci*, vol. 2, p. 33. The Fathers dressed as Buddhist monks until 1595, when they adopted the even more honorable dress of literati. On this matter, see Father Joseph Sebes, S.J., "A 'Bridge' between East and West: Father Matteo Ricci, S.J., His Times, His Life, and His Method of Cultural Accommodation," *International Symposium on Chinese-Western Cultural Interchange* (Taipei, 1983), pp. 588–92.

10. The phrase is in Latin.

11. Interpreters were Chinese recruited in Macao who knew some Western language and the Chinese vernacular. They were neither scholars nor converts. The behavior of the interpreters occasionally compromised the mission. See especially Ricci-Trigault, p. 143.

12. On Francesco Cabral, see Pfister, *Notices*, p. 18, and *Fonti Ricciane*, vol. 1, pp. 169–72. He was Superior of the China mission from early in 1583 to 1585, when he left Macao for Goa.

13. This is a confusing title and episode. A prefect summoned them to explain their status under the discredited *tu-t'ang*. They actually were under arrest without their knowledge. Eventually, by entreaty and bribery, they presented their case to the new *hai-tao* and *tu-t'ang*, who granted them the new permission and the land on which to build their house and church. On this, see Ricci-Trigault, pp. 140–44, and *Fonti Ricciane*, vol. 1, pp. 168–75. The Italian word given in the published text is *cocunfu* which seems to indicate a subprefect under a *tu-t'ang* or a mayor of a city, probably the city of Ansam.

14. This published version is a misleading abbreviation of the original letter as found in Tacchi Venturi, *Ricci*, vol. 2, p. 420. In the original Ruggieri explained that he could not obtain support in Macao because of the losses of Portuguese vessels, so he borrowed the money from Chinese friends. Ruggieri made no mention of a license to teach the Chinese, which in this published letter almost seems to be a way that the loan could be repaid.

15. This sentence does not appear in Ruggieri's original letter at all. That it was interpolated by an editor situated in Europe may explain why

the Italian ambiguously contrasts "here" to "here" (*qui* to *costì*). I translated the one as "there" in order to give sense to the text. However, since this is not Ruggieri's language, the determination is at best obscure.

16. In the original Ruggieri wrote of the "fear" that the Chinese have of Christians because of the reputation for bellicosity of the Portuguese and Spanish. He also recommended that great care be taken in the selection of other Fathers coming to China so that their conduct be beyond reproach. In Tachi Venturi, *Ricci*, vol. 2, p. 420.

17. These opening clauses are not found in the original letter.

18. On Ruggieri's literary studies and competence in Chinese letters and language, see Knud Lundbaek, "The First Translation from a Confucian Classic in Europe," *China Mission Studies Bulletin* 1 (1979), pp. 2–11.

19. For some reason the published version of the letter substituted *Madonna* for the *Nostra Signora* of the original. In Tacchi Venturi, *Ricci*, vol. 2, p. 422. Nor is *sacrificing* in the original letter.

20. Ruggieri did not use *baptize* in the original. He wrote that "for now we do not move to make Christians in order not to give any occasion to the Demon to demolish this new plant." In Tacchi Venturi, *Ricci*, vol. 2, p. 423. A further explanation of their caution at this time is given by Matteo Ricci in his journal: "In order that the appearance of a new religion might not arouse suspicion among the Chinese people, the Fathers did not speak openly about religious matters when they began to appear in public. What time was left to them, after paying their respects and civil compliments and courteously receiving their visitors, was spent in studying the language of the country, the methods of writing and the customs of the people. They did, however, endeavor to teach this pagan people in a more direct way, namely, by virtue of their example and the sanctity of their lives." Ricci-Trigault, p. 154. But even this text varies somewhat from the Ricci original as edited by D'Elia where the last part reads, "and move them by the good and exemplary life to that which they were neither able to do with language, nor did they have the time to do." *Fonti Ricciane*, vol. 1, p. 192.

21. The original of Ruggieri's letter goes on to say, "The lower and common people do not show much affection because they do not understand our life, which they wish would be like their's, dissolute in eating, drunkenness and other lasciviousness." Tacchi Venturi, *Ricci*, vol. 2, p. 424.

22. On the donor of these gilded tablets, Wang P'an, prefect of Chao

ch'ing and later *limsitao* of two provinces, see D'Elia, *Fonti Ricciane*, vol. 1, pp. 176, 199.

23. A picture of the originals of these two gilded plaques as preserved in the Jesuit Archives in Rome is to be found in Tacchi Venturi, *Ricci*, vol. 2, table 3; and in D'Elia, *Fonti Ricciane*, vol. 1, table 12. The pictures show the effort to translate these Chinese characters into Italian. I have given an English translation of that Italian as it was published in 1586. However, the Italian was incorrect, revealing the difficulty Ruggieri still had with reading Chinese characters. *Fonti Ricciane*, vol. 1, 199, recounts some of the difficulties they had in rendering the Chinese, and how subsequent scholarship has clarified the meaning. Father Joseph Sebes, in his previously cited 1983 article (see note 9), gives a definitive reading of the meaning of these inscriptions: "The prefect presented the establishment with two plaques, one reading Hsien-hua ssu (Fairy Flower Monastery), the other Hsi-lai ching-t'u (Pure Land from the West), both indicating that the Chinese at that time thought of the missionaries as Buddhists," p. 578. It is probable that Ruggieri himself did not understand the full meaning of the plaques. In fact, as my colleague Edwin J. Van Kley pointed out, the "Fairy" of the first title is a Taoist term which could also be rendered "Immortal." Surely, these subtleties of the language and its religious connotations escaped Ruggieri and his colleagues at the time. In the early decades of the seventeenth century, they would begin to discover them.

24. The problem of putting a Chinese poem into Latin accounts for some of the difficulty in getting at the precise meaning of these verses. I have been unable to discover what a "guò bird" is, but then maybe they didn't know either. That which Ruggieri's Latin conveys is that the Chinese saw Ruggieri and his companions as scholarly monks, devoted to prayer and learning. They came to China—"the region situated in the middle"—to seek truth and holiness. The "odor" of the last line refers again to their reputation for learning. The reader of the 1586 edition would probably not have sensed that the Chinese thought them to be Buddhists, and would only have read that the Jesuit Fathers were held in high esteem. I am grateful to my colleague Richard Wevers for assistance in translating this Latin poem.

25. This is the same Wang P'an, the prefect of Chao ch'ing. See note 22.

26. On this first Catechism, begun by Ruggieri in 1581 and the first book by a European printed in China in 1584, see *Fonti Ricciane*, vol. 1, pp. 197–98, and Tacchi Venturi, *Ricci*, vol. 2, pp. 498–540.

27. In the Italian text *lettera* and *lingua* are used. The usual distinction between these terms is that the first refers to the written characters of formal Chinese and the second refers to the spoken language. In this context the meaning seems to be that they observed the proprieties of Chinese written style and the language of the common people.

28. There is a serious difficulty with the text at this point. In the original letter, as published by Tacchi Venturi, *Ricci*, vol. 2, p. 51, the clause immediately following the statement about good letters and good idioms is: "assisted by some of their literati, we have accommodated to the reputation of the principle sects of China." In other words, the original letter suggested that the Catechism was written in the language of, and accommodated to the understanding of, the sects of China, whereas the published version stated that it refuted the teachings of those sects. A two-column comparison of the Italian texts shows the difference:

Published	*Original*
In quello si confutano le principali sette della Cina . . .	agiutati di alcuni suoi letterati, habbiamo accomodato con riputatione delle principali sette della Cina.

In the absence of the original manuscript, one cannot determine the accuracy of Tacchi Venturi's reading. There is a less commonly used Italian word, *refutatione*, which could have been Ruggieri's intended word, but it would still be strange that the European editor in 1586 changed it to *confutano* and eliminated *accomodato*. The more likely hypothesis is that the European editor thought his reading public would be more accepting of a Catechism written to refute Chinese teaching, than accommodated to it. Yet, in Ricci's original journal, edited by D'Elia, he wrote, "The Fathers accommodated a Catechism in these letters in which some points of the sects of China are refuted (*confutava*)." *Fonti Ricciane*, vol. 1, p. 197.

29. The map "in the manner of ours" placed China on the eastern edge. This seemed curious to the Chinese since on their maps China was the "Middle Kingdom" and centrally located. On this and later revisions by Ricci of what is known as his *Mappamondo*, see *Fonti Ricciane*, vol. 1, pp. 207–11.

30. Again, Wang P'an. See note 22.

31. That is, the devil or Satan.

32. The sentence is in Latin.

33. The Spanish original of this letter, in Tacchi Venturi, *Ricci*, vol.

2, p. 429, is clearer than the published Italian and has been used to translate this and other passages.

34. There are two discrepancies here between the original and the published versions of this sentence. In the original only two maps (*dos mapas*) were given rather than four. Further, the last clause in the Spanish says that other gifts were given to Father Ruggieri, who was his friend. Tacchi Venturi, *Ricci*, vol. 2, p. 429.

35. The last two sentences of this paragraph are not in the Spanish original.

36. This sentence is in Latin in the published version, but is not present in the Spanish original.

37. The Italian of the published text is confusing and has been clarified by the Spanish original. The map is that of Ricci. See notes 29 and 34.

38. This entire paragraph is not in the Spanish original letter and thus must be an interpolation by the European editor.

BIBLIOGRAPHY

Bibliography

he story of the Jesuit mission to China has often been told. It can be found in all histories of the Jesuit Order, and in all histories of Christian missions. Two books are particularly well suited to present the general background of these letters of 1583 and 1584. The first is George H. Dunne, S.J., *Generation of Giants: The Story of the Jesuits in China in the Last Decades of the Ming Dynasty*, Notre Dame: University of Notre Dame Press, 1962; and the second is Arnold H. Rowbotham, *Missionary and Mandarin: The Jesuits at the Court of China*, New York: Russell & Russell, 1966. C. W. Allan's *Jesuits at the Court of Peking*, Hong Kong & Shanghai: Kelly & Walsh, 1935; Pasquale D'Elia's *Catholic Missions in China: A Short Sketch of the History of the Catholic Church in China from the Earliest Records to Our Own Days*, Shanghai: Commercial Press, 1935; and Vincent Cronin's *The Wise Man from the West*, New York: Dutton, 1955, are among the older but still very useful books in English. The most recent and academically sound retelling of the immediate surrounding events is the brilliant article by Father Joseph Sebes, S.J., "A 'Bridge' between East and West: Father Matteo Ricci, S.J., His Time, His Life, and His Method of Cultural Accommodation," *International Symposium on Chinese-Western Cultural Interchange in Commemoration of the 400th Anniversary of the Arrival of Matteo Ricci, S.J., in China*, Taipei, 1983,

pp. 556–615. There is also a short work by Thomas F. Ryan, S.J., *Jesuits in China*, Hong Kong: Catholic Truth Society, 1964, which appeals to a general readership. The story is also competently told in Nigel Cameron, *Barbarians and Mandarins: Thirteen Centuries of Western Travelers in China*, New York: Walker/Weatherhill, 1970, pp. 149–94.

A periodical that regularly carries articles about the early Jesuit mission is *China Mission Studies (1550–1800)* Bulletin, vol. 1 (1979). One such article in that first volume is Knud Lundbaek's "The First Translation from a Confucian Classic in Europe," pp. 2–11. David Mungello routinely reports on sources and archives for the periodical.

Indispensable for an understanding of what Europeans knew about China in the sixteenth century is Donald F. Lach's *Asia in the Making of Europe*, vol. 1, *The Century of Discovery*, bks. 1 and 2, Chicago: University of Chicago Press, 1965. See especially bk. 1, pp. 314–31, on Jesuit letters and Letterbooks, and bk. 2, pp. 751–94 on the understanding of China following the 1585 publication in Rome of Juan González de Mendoza's *Historia de las cosas mas notables, ritos y costumbres del gran Reyno de la China*. An Italian edition of Mendoza was published in Venice in 1586, the same year as the letters in this volume.

For sound and clearly written descriptions of the China into which Ruggieri and his companions entered, see the three books by Charles O. Hucker: *The Traditional Chinese State in Ming Times (1368–1644)*, Tucson: University of Arizona Press, 1961; *The Censorial System of Ming China*, Stanford: Stanford University Press, 1966; and *The Ming Dynasty: Its Origins and Evolving Institutions*, Ann Arbor: University of Michigan Press, 1978. Since the Jesuit entry into China comes under the patronage of the Portuguese and their trading post in Macao, a very helpful study of that background is T'ien-Tse Chang's *Sino-Portuguese Trade from 1514 to 1644*, Leyden: E. J. Brill, 1969.

There is also available in English what is now commonly referred to as the journal of Matteo Ricci. After Ricci's death in 1610, his papers, consisting of letters and a diary, were taken by Nicholas Trigault. Trigault published the diary in a Latin edition in 1615, claiming to have amended and augmented Ricci's diary by material from his letters and those of others. This Trigault Latin version of Ricci's diary is now available in an English translation by Louis J. Gallagher, S.J., *China in the Sixteenth Century: The Journals of Matthew Ricci: 1583–1610*, New York: Random House, 1953. It is a fascinating document, but since it is a seventeenth-century "edited" version of Ricci it must be used with caution and compared with the twice-edited Italian original whenever possible.

The first to publish Ricci's original Italian text was Father Pietro Tacchi Venturi in *Le Opere Storiche del P. Matteo Ricci, S.J.*, 2 vols., Macerata: F. Giorgetti, 1911–13. For our purposes, the particular virtue of this work is that in volume 2 he edited manuscripts of the original letters of Ruggieri, Ricci, Pasio, and Cabral. A vastly expanded critical edition of Ricci's original diary, or journal, is Father Pasquale M. D'Elia, S.J., *Fonti Ricciane*, 3 vols., Rome: La Libreria Dello Stato, 1942–49. The erudition and critical scholarship of D'Elia make these volumes indispensable to anyone working in this area. Unfortunately, he never finished his projected editing of all the letters of Ricci and the others, and thus one must still use Tacchi Venturi for the letters.

There are two biobibliographical guides to the Jesuits in China. The older is that of P. Louis Pfister, S.J., *Notices Biographiques et Bibliographiques sur les Jésuites de l'Ancienne Mission de Chine: 1552–1773*, Chang-hai: La Mission Catholique, 1932. It is still essential to the scholar but must now be supplemented by the work of Joseph Dehergne, S.J., *Répertoire des Jésuites de Chine de 1552 à 1800*, Roma: Institutum Historicum S. I., 1973. Finally, the essential bibliography on the 1586 editions is that by Robert Streit, *Bibliotheca Missionum*, 22 vols., Munster, 1916– . In volume 4, Streit identifies four 1586 editions: one French published in Paris by Thomas Brumen; a German published in Dilingen by Joannem Mayer; and two Italian, one published in Rome by Francesco Zanetti and another in Venice by I. Gioliti. I have discovered at the Folger Shakespeare Library a third Italian edition done in Milan by Pacifico Pontio. The information on the title page is identical to the Zanetti edition except for the name and place of publication. Both editions end on page 188, but in the Zanetti edition the opposite page presents a list of *errori*, whereas the Pontio edition has this colophon: Registro / ABC-M / Tutti sono fogli. / In Milano / Per Pacifico Pontio, Impressore / della Corte Archiepiscop / MDLXXXVI.

The James Ford Bell Library at the University of Minnesota holds two of the three Italian editions of the 1586 Jesuit Letterbook from Japan. One is the edition published by Francesco Zanetti in Rome and presents the first letters from China on pages 169 to 188. The James Ford Bell Library's copy of this edition was used in the preparation of these translations. A facsimile of the title page of that copy is printed on page viii. The other edition in the Bell Library bears the Gioliti imprint.

This book is set in Garamond 49
with the display headings in Trajanus.
It is printed on Warren's Olde Style and
bound in Aiko Sugikawa with Holliston
Kingston around the spine. It was designed by
Gwen M. Willems of the University
of Minnesota Press. Of the limited
edition of 500 copies,
this is copy

———

9 780816 658589